Vincent van Gogh

He saw the world in vibrant colors

Written by
Amy Guglielmo

Illustrated by
Petra Braun

In 1853, a child named Vincent was born in the Dutch village of Zundert.
His parents were Anna and Theodorus van Gogh, a pastor.

Views from his childhood
home stayed with Vincent
his whole life—the church
steeple reaching for the sky,
neighbors working in the
fields, and families of magpies
nesting in the tall trees.

Vincent was the eldest of six children. The Van Gogh family enjoyed singing songs, reciting poetry, and reading fairytales. Vincent's mother had a fondness for the natural world. She liked to spend time outdoors with her family.

By day, Vincent walked the hills and looked at the flowers dotting the countryside. He played in the garden and built sandcastles with his siblings. In the evening, the family watched the sun set red behind the tall pines in the marsh. When Vincent returned home, he saw starlings resting on the church.

What do you see when you go for a walk outdoors?

Vincent's mother drew what she saw outdoors, filling her notebooks with sketches of flowers from her garden. Vincent also drew the things he saw as he walked through the woods, over the heath, and around the village. He was encouraged by his governess, who was the daughter of an artist.

Can you **sketch** the buildings near where you live? What **shapes** are they?

On some special occasions, Vincent gave his parents a drawing as a present. Vincent's parents appreciated their son's drawings as thoughtful gifts. They encouraged Vincent's interest in art, but no one imagined he would go on to become an artist!

When Vincent was 11, he was sent away to boarding school. Vincent felt sad. He would miss the sandy streets and the muddy farms of home. He would miss the marsh and the birds he heard whistling in the cemetery beside his house. Most of all, he would miss his family, especially his little brother Theo, who was his best friend.

It was a rainy autumn day when Vincent's father dropped him off a school in Zevenbergen. Vincent stoo on the school steps and waved as the yellow carriage bumped away. He looked up at the tall buildings and down at the muddy street. Vincent was only 20 miles from home, but he felt very alone.

After two years, Vincent moved to a new high school in a grand building that had once been a royal palace. One of Vincent's teachers was a painter named Cornelius C. Huysmans. Vincent had art lessons with the rest of his classmates, but these were only a small portion of his life at school.

Do you like to draw at school?

Try drawing your classroom or classmates.

Vincent also studied Dutch, German, French, English, arithmetic, history, geography, botany, zoology, calligraphy, and gymnastics! He received particularly good grades in languages. But he quit the school halfway through his second year, never to return.

When Vincent turned 16, he began
training as a dealer at an art gallery
in the bustling city of The Hague.
The gallery was an elegant building
with ornate curtains. Its walls were
crowded with gold-framed prints
and paintings that hung all the
way to the ceiling.

Vincent was eager to learn his new trade. He did so well that he was soon making more money than his father. Vincent could not get enough of the art. Even in his free time, he spent hours looking at it. On his days off, he visited museums in Amsterdam and saw great works of art by the Dutch masters Rembrandt van Rijn, Johannes Vermeer, and Frans Hals.

When Theo came to visit, Vincent showed him the art he adored. The brothers made a promise to always keep in touch through letters.

After Vincent finished his training, he was sent
to London to learn more about the art business.
He bought a top hat and fancy gloves to celebrate!
The energy and sights of the city dazzled him.

Everywhere Vincent looked in London, there were interesting things to see—neat flower beds, people on horseback, and children playing in the park. In his spare time, Vincent loved visiting art museums and galleries. At night, he read poetry, literature, and books about artists. He wrote to Theo and told him about all he saw.

Try drawing a busy city scene or a park full of people.
What details can you spot?

However, after a year or two, Vincent fell out of love with London. His mood grew gloomy and his work suffered. Vincent's family noticed that his letters were no longer as happy and excited as they had once been. Vincent was transferred to work in a Paris gallery to make a fresh start.

In Paris, Vincent visited exhibitions and the Louvre museum, but even with all this new art to see, he wasn't happy. Vincent grew grouchy and began to act oddly. He left his workplace without permission and argued with the customers.

Finally, his employers told him to leave. Enough was enough!

Searching for a new calling, Vincent decided he would become a pastor, like his father.

He returned to England, where he took jobs as a teacher.
One school allowed him to live there for free while he studied
to become a pastor. Vincent began preaching sermons in the
local church. He told Theo he felt happy when he was preaching.

Vincent sent letters to Theo
with sketches of the view from
his window—his school, a lamppost,
and the curving driveway where
the students said goodbye
to their parents.

What can you see
from your window?

Vincent soon grew homesick. His uncle, a minister, agreed to help him prepare for a special exam. If he passed the exam, he could become a pastor. Vincent moved to Amsterdam to begin studying. However, he spent more time exploring the city and surrounding countryside. His uncle advised Vincent to try something else.

So Vincent left to become a missionary in the coal fields of Belgium.
The struggles of the mine workers he saw there moved him deeply.
To show sympathy for them, he gave up most of his belongings and
lived in a hut with a small straw mattress. He made sketches of bleak
landscapes and soot-covered miners carrying heavy bags of coal.
Vincent drew what he saw, but he didn't see himself as an artist yet.

Watch people on their way to work.
Try drawing them!

After only six months, Vincent was fired from his job. The church did not approve of his disheveled appearance and odd behaviors! Sad and dispirited, Vincent was not sure what to do next. In his letters to Theo, Vincent asked his brother for support and advice.

Theo sent money to help Vincent pay for food and lodgings, but that wasn't all. He also sent drawing materials and suggested that his brother should become a professional artist. At first, Vincent wasn't sure. Until now, he had drawn purely for pleasure. Would people really pay for his pictures?

Vincent felt encouraged by his brother's support and sent him drawings for feedback. Theo now had a good job as an art dealer himself. Vincent hoped the brothers could work together—maybe Theo could even help Vincent sell his work!

Vincent wrote back: *"I'll pick up my pencil ... and I'll get back to drawing ..."*

Vincent

Eager to develop his art skills, Vincent moved to Brussels in 1880. There, he copied prints by famous artists, practiced perspective drawings, and enrolled in classes to draw live models. He met other artists and read every human anatomy book he could find! Vincent was only in Brussels for six months, but he continued to practice and develop these skills for many years to come.

Look closely at your hand. Try drawing it in different positions.

When he again ran out of money, Vincent moved to stay with his parents in the Dutch countryside in Etten. He made lots of drawings of people working in the fields. In his artworks, Vincent tried to show the dignity of these hardworking diggers, sowers, and planters.

During this time, Vincent experimented with many different materials, such as pencil and charcoal, chalk, pen and ink, and watercolor paints.

City life again beckoned to Vincent. This time, he was off to The Hague to take lessons from his cousin, the artist Anton Mauve. Using carefully chosen pigments, chalk, and ink, Vincent drew city views and made endless figure drawings. He worked tirelessly, practicing in the studio nearly every day.

Up until now, Vincent had concentrated on drawing. It was Mauve who taught Vincent how to be a painter. He also taught him about light and shadow. Because Mauve painted in tones of gray, green, and blue, Vincent did, too, using watercolors and oil paints to capture what he saw.

Sadly, the cousins' arrangement didn't last.
Mauve and Vincent had many arguments about art,
about money, and about life. The two parted ways.

Experiment
_by painting with a
restricted palette of
colors, as Mauve did._

Not long after this, Vincent received his first commission: 12 cityscapes from his uncle Cor, an art dealer. Vincent also sent more drawings to his brother Theo. With Theo's encouragement and support, Vincent continued to develop his artistic skills.

The cityscapes did not lead to any further paid work.
Vincent found himself drawn back to nature. He traveled
to the Dutch province Drenthe to paint the heathland
and the women working on the peat moors.
When he ran out of money, he slept outside
and traded drawings for food.

Eventually, this lonely life was too much even for Vincent.
After three months in the rain and cold, Vincent once
again went to live with his parents, now in a village named
Nuenen. But he did not give up drawing or painting!

Nuenen, Vincent worked even harder. preparation for a single painting, made dozens of practice versions. missed meals and sleep because he s spending so much time on his art.

Try drawing the same image over and over again, as Vincent did.

ncent sent his portrait studies to eo, hoping that he might be able sell them in Paris. Unfortunately, eo knew Vincent's dark tones re not colorful enough to attract e attention of buyers.

But Vincent persisted, enrolling at the academy of art in Antwerp. He was enchanted with the models, materials, and museums, but he found the classes too traditional. Vincent knew he was different from the other students. He longed to try something fresh and new.

In 1886, Vincent joined Theo in Paris. There, he met artists—known as the Impressionists and Post-Impressionists—who were using bold colors and brushstrokes to capture a scene. It was a whole new way of painting! Vincent took inspiration from artists Theo introduced him to, including Edgar Degas, Camille Pissarro, and Claude Monet. He also made friends with Henri de Toulouse-Lautrec and Emile Bernard. He began painting with a lighter, brighter palette and experimenting with different methods.

Vincent and Theo collected hundreds of Japanese woodblock prints, which Vincent copied. He also focused on portrait painting. When he couldn't afford a model, he just painted himself. While in Paris, Vincent made more than 20 self-portraits! Once again, Vincent hoped to sell his paintings. He even organized exhibitions. But once again, people weren't very interested in buying them.

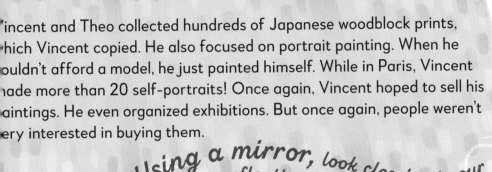

Using a mirror, look closely at your reflection. Draw what you see.

Vincent didn't enjoy the winters in Paris. They were dark and cold. He longed to paint outside in the bright sun. He moved to Arles, in the south of France, and hoped other artists would join him there. Only one artist was persuaded. Paul Gauguin moved into the yellow house that was Vincent's home and studio.

In Arles, Vincent painted everything he saw around him. He painted the dazzling countryside, the yellow house, and his bedroom. He painted ordinary objects, such as shoes on the red-tiled floor of his house.

He painted in cafés, in the street, in the park, on riverbanks, in the fields, and in the middle of the night. He carefully considered everything he saw before he put his brush to the canvas and began painting.

Study your shoes.
Try painting them **quickly!**

His colors were now more vivid and his brushstrokes confident. He sometimes applied paint so thickly, it took weeks to dry. Vincent made hundreds of paintings. He liked to finish a painting in one go, then move on to the next!

Vincent wanted to be known as the painter of sunflowers. Something about their bold, unfussy forms really attracted him. Before Gauguin's arrival, Vincent decorated his friend's room with his paintings, including pictures of sunflowers.

Gauguin and Vincent painted side by side, indoors and outdoors, each learning from the other. Gauguin made a portrait of Vincent painting his favorite flowers. Vincent painted pictures of both artists' chairs.

What do you see when you look at a sunflower?

But after a few weeks, Gauguin and Vincent began to bicker.
They had very different views on art. Gauguin believed in painting
from his imagination, while Vincent preferred painting what he saw.

Following one particular disagreement, Gauguin announced that he was
leaving. Vincent became so distressed that he cut off a piece of his ear.
Vincent was taken to the hospital, where Theo rushed to visit him.

Upon his return to the yellow house, Vincent kept painting. He created several still-life pictures and two self-portraits with his freshly bandaged ear. He painted the people he saw, such as his doctor, and also continued work on a series of portraits of his local postmaster, Joseph Roulin, and his wife, Augustine Roulin.

But soon Vincent's neighbors grew wary of his unsettled behavior and asked him to leave.

Throughout his life, Vincent experienced many symptoms of physical and mental illness. To help him get better, he volunteered to enter a hospital.

He was given a spare room to use as a studio so he could keep painting. Vincent painted what he saw: the hallways, irises from the gardens, cypress trees, and even fellow patients. During his yearlong stay, he made more than 150 paintings, including one of his most famous—*Starry Night*.

One day, Vincent received a special announcement. He had a new nephew and namesake: Theo's baby Vincent! He made a painting called *Almond Blossom* to celebrate the new arrival.

While Vincent was in the hospital, six of his paintings were shown in Brussels and one of them was sold! At last, people were starting to take notice of Vincent's art and his unique style. After leaving the hospital, Vincent moved to live closer to Theo, who was in Paris. Vincent moved to an artists' village, Auvers-sur-Oise, under the care of Dr. Paul Gachet. There, he painted day and night. He completed 70 paintings in 70 days.

Try painting **night** *and* **daytime** *scenes. What difference do you see?*

Vincent was spending more and more time in the fields. At first, it seemed to be doing him good.

But soon, Vincent's health suffered once more. Vincent died of a self-inflicted gunshot wound to the chest, aged just 37. He took his final breath in the arms of his brother Theo.

Vincent was dead, but his art was not.
His paintings remained, blazing with color
and life. Shortly after Vincent's death,
Theo held a memorial exhibition of his work.

Sadly, not long after the show, Theo also
passed away. His widow Jo was left with
hundreds of Vincent's paintings and letters.
She was advised to get rid of them all!
But Jo was determined to keep the work
of both Theo and Vincent alive.

o set down the family history and arranged
many exhibitions of Vincent's work. The art
world was changing, and people were seeing
things with fresh eyes. Vincent's paintings
sparked interest across Europe, and people
talked excitedly about his work.

Jo also published a book of the
brothers' letters. More people
sought to buy Vincent's work and
read about his life. Other artists
began to borrow ideas from
Vincent's style.

*What do you
like most about
Vincent's work?*

Following Jo's death, care of the Van Gogh art collection passed to her son, Vincent's nephew and namesake. He felt strongly that Vincent's groundbreaking work should be on view for everyone to see, for all time, so he helped create the Van Gogh Museum in Amsterdam. It opened in 1973.

In his brief lifetime, Vincent made nearly 900 paintings and 1,100 works on paper. While he was living, these works went mostly unappreciated.

Today, the world sees Vincent van Gogh as one of the greatest and most original artists of all time. The years he spent studying, practicing, and developing as an artist is recognized and admired. He is considered a genius, a trailblazer, and a pioneer of modern art.

"When my life is over, all I hope is that I shall depart it looking back with love and wistfulness and thinking: oh the paintings I might have made!"

–Vincent van Gogh, 1883

Timeline of key artworks

Most of Vincent van Gogh's nearly 900 paintings and 1,100 works on paper were completed between 1881 and 1890. Here are a few of his key works from that time, all in the collection of The Metropolitan Museum of Art.

1881 Road in Etten
Chalk

1885 Peasant Woman Cooking by a Fireplace
Oil on canvas

1885 The Potato Peeler (reverse: Self-Portrait with a Straw Hat)
Oil on canvas

"People say ... that it's difficult to know oneself—but it's not easy to paint oneself either."

–Vincent van Gogh, 1889

1887 Sunflowers
Oil on canvas

1887 Self-Portrait with a Straw Hat
Oil on canvas

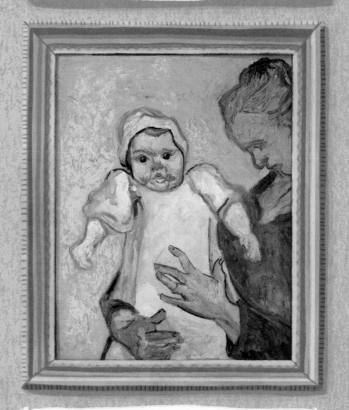

1888 Madame Roulin and Her Baby
Oil on canvas

Timeline continued:

1888 *Shoes*
Oil on canvas

1889 *Olive Trees*
Oil on canvas

1889 *Wheat Field with Cypresses*
Oil on canvas

1889 Corridor in the Asylum
Oil on canvas

1890 Irises
Oil on canvas

1890 First Steps, after Millet
Oil on canvas

"How rich art is. If one can remember what one has seen, one is never empty of thoughts or truly lonely, never alone."

–Vincent van Gogh, 1878

Make a self-portrait

Using bright, bold colors and short brushstrokes, Vincent van Gogh used a painting technique that he called "color gymnastics." He painted more than 35 self-portraits in his unique style, including several that include him wearing different hats.

Vincent painted this self-portrait in Paris. At this time in his career, he was still developing his own style. He repeated the same exercises again and again for practice. Vincent even reused old canvases to save money. This painting was done on the back of another picture!

Self-Portrait with a Straw Hat, 1887, oil on canvas

Try this yourself!

Now it's your turn!
Before you create your masterpiece, consider wearing a signature piece of clothing or including something like a favorite hat to make it represent you.

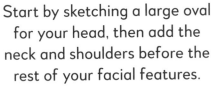

Start by sketching a large oval for your head, then add the neck and shoulders before the rest of your facial features.

Work with a mirror next to you so you can look at your reflection for reference while you draw.

For a bigger challenge, try to paint a series of 20, like Van Gogh did in Paris! You could try wearing different outfits, too.

Paint, paint, and paint again!

Vincent van Gogh painted many still lifes so that he could experiment with color. A still life is a work of art observing an arrangement of objects, like fruit or flowers. Vincent is famous for painting sunflowers, but he also painted different types of flowers in different vases and with different-colored backgrounds. He even painted sunflower heads where the flowers had faded and started going to seed.

"I find comfort in contemplating the sunflowers."

–Vincent van Gogh, 1883

Sunflowers, 1887, oil on canvas

ow you have a go:
or this project, pick an
em or group of items
at interests you and
rrange it in front of
ou. You can draw your
rrangement using
ens, pencils, pastels,
r use paints.

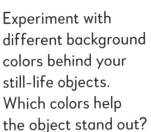

Experiment with
different background
colors behind your
still-life objects.
Which colors help
the object stand out?

Irises, 1890, oil on canvas

Challenge
yourself!

Use a mix of objects that you
might have nearby. Practice
getting the size of each object
right in comparison to the others.

Oleanders, 1888, oil on canvas

You don't have to paint flowers!
Why not try drawing a selection
of shoes belonging to you or
your family? Capture the
details of the laces, soles,
and floor beneath them.

Shoes, 1887, oil on canvas

Glossary

calligraphy (*noun*)
Decorative handwriting or lettering generally
created with a quill, pen, or brush.

Impressionists (*noun*)
A group of late 19th-century artists who painted scenes
of everyday life with lively brushwork and vivid color and
paid special attention to the changing effects of light.

modern art (*noun*)
Art created from approximately the 1860s through
the 1970s. Modern artists rejected traditional
techniques of the past in the spirit of experimentation.

perspective drawing (*noun*)
A type of painting or drawing that makes
some objects appear closer than others.

pigment (*noun*)
The part of paint, usually a powder, that gives it
color when mixed with oil, water, or another fluid.

Post-Impressionists (*noun*)
Artists who stretched the boundaries of Impressionism by
intensifying color and form for less naturalistic and more expressive
effects, aiming to give their work greater substance and meaning.

self-portrait (*noun*)
Artwork that an artist makes of their own likeness.

still life (*noun*)
A painting or drawing of an arrangement of objects,
such as flowers in a vase, fruit in a bowl, or a pair of shoes.

About the author

Amy Guglielmo is an author, artist, arts educator, and an arts advocate. She has written many books for children, including *Cezanne's Parrot* and *Just Being Dalí: The Story of Artist Salvador Dalí*. Amy has co-authored the picture books *Pocket Full of Colors: The Magical World of Mary Blair*, winner of the Christopher Award; *How to Build a Hug: Temple Grandin and Her Amazing Squeeze Machine*; and the *Touch the Art* series of novelty board books featuring famous works of art with tactile additions. She lives on Lake Champlain with her husband.

About the artist

Petra Braun is an artist and illustrator living in the countryside of Austria. She has studied Graphic Design and holds a degree in Fine Arts/Painting. She has now found her love for illustration and creates most of her work digitally. Like Vincent, she loves to draw outside in nature, so she often can be found at a quiet spot beside the river next to her house, drawing on her iPad.

Senior Editor Emma Grange
Senior Designer Anna Formanek
Project Editor Beth Davies
Editor Julia March
Designer Zoë Tucker
Picture Researchers Martin Copeland,
Sumedha Chopra, and Sumita Khatwani
Production Editor Siu Yin Chan
Senior Production Controller Lloyd Robertson
Managing Editor Paula Regan
Managing Art Editor Jo Connor
Publishing Director Mark Searle

First American Edition, 2021
Published in the United States by DK Publishing
1450 Broadway, Suite 801, New York, NY 10018

Page design copyright © 2021 Dorling Kindersley Limited
DK, a Division of Penguin Random House LLC
21 22 23 24 25 10 9 8 7 6 5 4 3 2 1
001–322694–Aug/2021

The Metropolitan
Museum of Art
New York

© The Metropolitan Museum of Art

A catalog record for this book
is available from the Library of Congress.
ISBN 978-0-7440-3366-3

DK books are available at special discounts when purchased in bulk for sales
promotions, premiums, fund-raising, or educational use. For details, contact:
DK Publishing Special Markets,
1450 Broadway, Suite 801, New York, NY 10018
SpecialSales@dk.com

Printed and bound in China

Acknowledgments
DK would like to thank Susan Stein, Lisa Silverman Meyers,
Laura Barth, Leanne Graeff, Emily Blumenthal, and Morgan Pearce
at The Met; Hilary Becker; Clare Baggaley; Julie Ferris and Lisa
Lanzarini; Kayla Dugger; and Amy Guglielmo and Petra Braun.
The author would like to thank the colorful Dietschi family.

For the curious

www.dk.com
www.metmuseum.org